## Chapter 1: Cricut Basics

To grow your inventive skylines and make your own stickers, welcoming cards, names, paper blossoms, texture iron-ons, and the sky is the limit from there, Cricut is the ideal device. An electronic machine, there are many models (which we'll get into later in this section), yet they all are planned for creating of all kinds.

### What is Cricut?

First off, what is Cricut precisely? It's a brilliant cutting machine (Cricut is the brand name) fit for cutting a wide range of plans into an immense assortment of materials like felt, card stock, and that's only the tip of the iceberg, which you embed into the machine like you would paper into a printer. Cricut is simply recreating your hand-cutting abilities with advanced accuracy. Cricut can likewise draw and compose with an assortment of pen styles (metallic, gel, sparkle, fine-point, and so on) providing your activities with the comfortable feel of penmanship, just substantially more exact. Cricut can likewise score material for simple collapsing, which you really want for cards.

While it's anything but a printer, Cricut makes them print abilities, kind of. There's a Print Then Cut capacity, which you would use for projects like stickers. The Cricut programming sends pictures your home printer, it prints out, and afterward you use Cricut to make your cuts. We'll get into how that capacity functions in a later chapter.

Different models accompany somewhat unique additional items, however generally speaking, all Cricuts have the following:

- The genuine cutting machine unit
- A fine-point sharp edge and edge housing
- A LightGrip cutting mat
- A power adapter
- A USB cable
- Materials for a training project
- Access to Design Space

How does Cricut play out this large number of errands? Programming. In particular, the Cricut Design Space programming. This opens up the universe of Cricut and every one of the tasks that are conceivable. We'll get into everything programming in a later part, however for the time being, simply realize that Design Space is the center point of your Cricut machine. You pick the kind of undertaking you need to do and fabricate your design.

A speedy note on an actual component that used to be available, yet isn't any longer: cartridges. These aren't similar to ink cartridges, in light of the fact that Cricut isn't a printer.
Cartridges were sets of pictures and textual styles. They cost between $5-$30, but

now, Cricut is absolutely computerized. To assist with the change, fresher models are frequently viable with actual cartridges, yet not needed. Every one of the textual styles and pictures are currently accessible through Cricut Design Space online.

**Cricut models**

There are many Cricut models out there and relying upon what your creative desires are, certain models are superior to other people. How about we take a look:

The Cricut Explore One

Cricut markets this machine as the "most reasonable passage point." This model can cut, compose, and score 100 materials. It's viable with Cricut cartridges, in the event that you have some from more established models. The cutting edge is a fine-point and the machine is viable with devices like the Scoring Stylus and Deep-Point Blade, which you'll need to purchase independently. At the cost (around $250, when not on special), you prepare 25 to-make ventures to begin and material for your first undertaking. The principle disadvantage to the Explore One is that it can't be associated through Bluetooth, so you really want to interface your gadget (the Design Space programming is viable with iOS, Android, Windows, and Mac) with a rope. It additionally is certainly not a twofold instrument cartridge, which implies you can't compose and cut (or score and cut) at one at once; to do one, set the material back into the machine, and do the other one.

Cricut Explore Air and Air 2

Also actually reasonable, the Explore Air and Air 2 are remote, with a shrewd dial for profundity and tension. The enormous distinction between them is the Air 2 has a Fast Mode and a bigger body. Like the Explore One, both can cut 100 materials and utilize a fine-point edge. The Fast Mode permits the machine to slice up to 2x occasions quicker. Assuming that you have a great deal of slicing to do, this is particularly valuable. The Design

Space programming works for iOS, Android, Windows, and Mac, and the Air 2 is viable with Cricut cartridges.

<u>Circuit Maker</u>

The most current Cricut machine, Maker is a great new individual from the Circuit family. It can cut unbonded texture and thicker materials like balsa wood and cowhide utilizing the Knife Blade. That implies it can cut an incredible 300 materials. Rather than the Scoring Stylus, Maker can utilize the Scoring Wheel, so more material sorts can be scored. At the point when you purchase the machine on the Cricut site, you get a revolving sharp edge and fine-point edge, fine point pen, two cutting mats, and 50 prepared to-make projects. It's additionally viable with a large group of independently sold devices like QuickSwap apparatuses for fast changes between scoring, engraving, etc. The Cricut Maker has a Fast Mode, as well. It's a fairly expensive machine at around $400.

**Buying considerations**

So, which of the Cricut models would it be advisable for you to get? There a few contemplations you should ponder before committing:

<u>Cutting speed</u>

How quick does the Cricut display do its thing? The better quality ones like Explore Air 2 and the Maker have a Fast Mode, which surrenders you velocities to twice quicker. Assuming creating is only a great leisure activity, you probably won't require that speed, yet on the off chance that you really want to produce a high volume, speed will likely matter.

<u>Wireless/not wireless</u>

How significant is a remote Cricut to you? Assuming you have an assigned creating space and space for the machine, you may be thoroughly cool with connecting your gadget and shipping off plans to the machine. Assuming that space is an issue, notwithstanding, remote may be what you like. Actually take a look at the model particulars prior to settling on your decision. The Explore One can be turned remote with the Bluetooth Adapter.

<u>Materials</u>

Cricuts can cut somewhere around 100 materials, with the Maker dominating at 300. Assuming you utilize a specific material like cowhide, you need to check and be certain that the Cricut you need can deal with it. Assuming you just arrangement on utilizing cardstock and other paper, one of the fledgling

Cricuts will presumably be great enough.

<u>Accessories</u>

Cricuts accompany a couple of additional items, however they can truly grow when you get independently sold instruments like various blades and pens. Few out of every odd pen or blade is viable with each machine, so consistently discover what you can add to your Cricut prior to picking it. Cricut will likewise sell groups, so when taking a gander at a model, check whether there's a pack accessible that is worth it.

<u>Your imaginative style</u>

Taken all together, the contemplations above fundamentally reduce to your creative style. Contemplate what your making enthusiasm is and what you truly need (and need) from a machine. Assuming you center around making your own hello cards, you presumably won't require a machine like the Maker, since you won't

utilize by far most of materials it's fit for cutting. Assuming velocity is a thought, you will likely need a model with a Fast Speed mode. Possibly you're zeroing in on explicit ventures at this moment, however need the choice to extend with embellishments or materials. Taking into account what you like to do can assist you with concluding which machine is the best fit.

## Chapter 2: What A Cricut Can Do

So we realized what a Cricut machine is and the distinctive model choices, however for what reason would it be advisable for you to get one? What would you be able to definitely make with a Cricut? Before we dive into more detail on programming, plan, and really utilizing the machine, how about we stop and go over the making possibilities.

**What Cricuts can cut**

Cricut's Explore Series can cut 100 or so materials, while the most current Maker can hit 300. Here are a portion of the materials, to provide you with a thought of what you need to work with:

Paper Card
stock
Construction paper
Wrapping paper
Parchment paper
Wax paper
Tattoo    paper

Sticker   paper
Tissue paper
Paper staple sacks
Photo paper
Poster board
Vinyl (paper, iron-on, sparkle, window-stick, dry-erase)
Fabric (silk, denim, felt, false softened cowhide, artificial calfskin, wool, cloth, burlap, cotton)
Velvet (Maker just)
Moleskin (Maker just)
Fleece (Maker just)
Washi paper and tape
Cord board
Cardboard Cereal
boxes Rice paper
Watercolor paper
Craft froth
Aluminum foil
Sheet pipe tape
Magnetic sheets
Canvas
Birch wood (of specific thickness)
Balsa wood
Chipboard (of certain thickness)
Aluminum metal (of specific thickness)
Stencil film
Transparency film

**What you can make with Cricut**

You can make apparently incalculable artworks with a Cricut machine, and later in this book, we'll walk you through how to make a couple of them. Pretty much any sort of individual can track down motivation to utilize Cricut. Regardless of whether you're an expert craftsman who needs to get your work on stickers or decals; an educator who needs to make redid stickers for understudies; or a scrapbooker who's worn out on removing everything the hard way, Cricut can help. In the event that you don't know what you would involve a Cricut for, here's a rundown of what's possible:

Shapes and lettering for scrapbooks
Christmas cards
Customized   present

labels       Christmas
adornments Signs
Customized caps
Keychains
Bookmarks
Pillow cases
Bullet diary
craftsmanship
Nail
workmanship
stickers
Wedding solicitations
Wedding cake designs
Customized handbags
Halloween decorations
Picture book representations and
message Leather bracelets
Leather studs
Personalized magnets
Customized T-shirts
Stencils
Vinyl stickers for windows
Pantry labels
Coasters
Iron-on patches for pants
Stickers
Wall decals
Quilt squares

**Other suggested supplies**

Before beginning your first Cricut projects, it's really smart to have a few Cricut embellishments and general making supplies available, other than the material you're utilizing for the Cricut, obviously. Contingent upon your venture, the helpful supplies will fluctuate, yet they could include:

<u>Cricut pens</u>

There are so many pen choices out there, so it truly relies upon the look you need. There are metallic pens, fine-point, gel, sparkle, extra-fine, calligraphy, launderable, and more.

Obviously, pens are in each shade of the rainbow, also. Cricut are utilized for drawing and composing. We'll speak more with regards to them as they become pertinent to explicit projects.

<u>Weeder</u>

If your task includes vinyl, you'll require a weeder. This little picking apparatus allows you to clear off abundance vinyl bits, so your plan truly pops.

<u>Grip mats</u>

Your Cricut will accompany one guide, likely the LightGrip one, which is really great for most paper. To work with thicker material, you'll require a studier mat.

The StandardGrip works for most materials, aside from presumably the thickest ones. You'll require the StrongGrip for stuff like chipboard, artificial cowhide, etc. All Cricut mats come in two sizes: 12 x 12-inches and 12 x 24-inches.

<u>Extra blades</u>

Different materials require various edges. The one your machine doubtlessly accompanies will not have the option to handle thick materials, so you ought to get the Deep Point or the Maker-explicit Knife Blade.

There's additionally a fine-direct sharp edge for extra complex work on light-toward medium weight materials; a fortified texture edge; thus on.

<u>Scoring tool</u>

If you need to make a card with score lines, so it's not difficult to crease, you really want a scoring stylus.

A scoring instrument allows you to make overlap lines for cards, boxes, envelopes, etc. For the Maker, the Scoring Wheel is new. It resembles the pointer, however updated, so it can score a more extensive scope of materials.

Both the pointer and wheel are sold

independently. <u>Heat press</u>

For projects that expect you to apply heat, similar to press on vinyl, you'll require some sort of hotness press. Many individuals simply utilize an iron, nonetheless there are committed machines expected for more tricky purposes. Cricut even sells their own; they call it EasyPress. They can be really expensive, so assuming that you don't anticipate utilizing it a ton, you can presumably stay with an ordinary iron. The advantage of a machine like the EasyPress, however, is that it's simpler to press on strange shapes. An ordinary iron isn't actually flexible.

<u>Good glue</u>

When Cricut has wrapped up cutting your undertaking, it's your chance to get to work. For a great deal of ventures (like scrapbooks and cards), you'll gather the cut pieces.

A decent paste is required. Ensure it's intended for the material you're

utilizing. <u>Ruler</u>

If you create by any means, you most likely as of now have a ruler. In the event that you don't, go out and get one. You presumably needn't bother with a very extravagant one, so whatever is reasonable and appears to be tough is fine.

<u>Scissors</u>

Even however Cricut is doing the greater part of cutting for you, you'll doubtlessly still need scissors. Get a couple intended for the material you'll use, since a material like texture is entirely different than, for instance, cardstock.

## Chapter 3: How To Get Started With Design Space

Let's say you have all that you want to begin: how would you really do it? In this part, we'll go through setting up your machine and taking an inside and out book at Design Space, Cricut's war room for making every one of your undertakings. We should begin with simply getting the machine out.

### Setting up the machine

Get your Cricut machine and placed in the spot you've picked. Assuming it's remote, it can go essentially anyplace you have space (as long as it's inside 10-15 feet of your associated gadget), yet on the off chance that it should be connected, pick where that is not difficult to do. Plug in the machine and (if essential) plug the Cricut into your gadget by means of USB link. Assuming it's a Bluetooth association, the Cricut should be turned on, and you'll should be certain your gadget's Bluetooth is empowered. You can interface the Cricut to the gadget by going to the gadget's settings and opening "Gadgets." Hit "Bluetooth." The gadget should detect the Cricut machine and permit you to choose it. Contingent upon the particular gadget you're utilizing, arrangement might be marginally unique, yet that is the jist of it.

Next, it's an ideal opportunity to go into the Cricut Design Space. It's a cloud-put together programming accessible with respect to programs, and there's additionally a sidekick application, so you can plan in a hurry. It's allowed to utilize on the off chance that you're transferring and utilizing your own pictures, and no membership to Cricut Access is expected to cut. Bloggers and crafters will regularly make their work of art/text accessible free of charge to download and transfer, as well. To get sufficiently close to all that Cricut brings to the table, which incorporates admittance to many text styles, pictures and selective arrangements and deals on premium text styles/pictures/projects, you should pay either a month to month membership or a yearly fee.

When you initially go to Cricut, you'll have to make another client profile. Click on the New Machine Setup. Assuming you have a Cricut account as of now, you can simply sign in. For new clients, follow the headings on the screen. You will be approached to download and introduce a Design Space plugin.

To introduce Design Space through an application, ensure the gadget is matched with your Cricut machine, and afterward download the application. Open it up, and sign in or make your ID. Hit "Menu" and afterward "Machine Setup and App Overview." Select "New Machine Setup" and follow the directions.

For both program and application arrangements, you know all that worked when you're approached to begin making a new project.

**Navigating Design Space**

You're in! You are currently inside an area called "Material." If you've at any point utilized Photoshop or any sort of media altering programming or application, this will seem recognizable. You plan inside a framework, and on the menus around it, you make choices to transfer or purchase pictures and textual styles, assemble and change plans, and afterward tell your Cricut to cut.

To stroll through Design Space, we alluded to DayDream Into Reality's blog entry regarding the matter, where she meticulously described the situation on what each symbol implies. We'll shorten it here, however look at Catalina's post "Full Cricut Design Space Tutorial For Beginners – 2019" to find out additional. How about we start with the overall material region, since it's the biggest:

*Canvas framework - It's the network where you plan, and you can turn the lattice lines off or on.* The matrix lines can assist you with envisioning what the cuts will really resemble on your chose material.

*Measurements - You can change estimations from creeps to cm (and turn the framework on/off) by tapping on the top board switch and afterward Settings.*

*Zoom - Zoom in or out on the grid.*

That's all fundamental, so how about we move to the

Top board. <u>Top</u>

On the highest point of the screen, you'll see every one of the symbols utilized for altering and organizing. Here, you can pick textual styles, sizes, move stuff around, etc. You'll likewise have the option to move around inside Design Space to your profile and tasks. There's a "Save" symbol, too, which is vital and ought to be clicked often; and a radiant green "Make it" button. That is the thing that you'll hit when you're completely set in Canvas and need to send the venture off to the Cricut to be cut. On the left of that button, you should see the name (Explore, Explore Air 2, Maker) of your Cricut machine there. You need to be certain that the name is really what your machine is.

Now, how about we drop down a little. This board seems to be like what you'd find in a Word report, with terms like "Text style," "Style,etc. From this menu, you'll have the option to assemble and change what's in your Canvas. Here is a fast summary of the symbols. A great deal of them are obvious, so we'll be as

brief as possible.

*Undo/re-try - A standard altering device to fix an error or re-try something.*

*Linetype -* This tells Cricut what action you want to apply, i.e. "cut," "draw," and "score." If you have the Maker, you'll have more options. It's important to know which one to choose, so you don't end up saying a line should be "cut" when you really wanted it to be a "score." "Cut" is the default linetype, so be sure to change it as needed. When you choose "draw," you'll be asked to choose from the available Cricut pens.

*Fill - This possibly actuates when you pick 'Cut' as your linetype.* "Fill" is utilized for the most part for printing and examples, so on the off chance that you're not anticipating printing first from Design Space, you can simply pick "No Fill."

*Print - The other choice adjacent to "No Fill" is Print.* This implies, when you hit "Make It," the plan is shipped off your home printer first. We'll get into this interaction later on, however for the time being, simply realize that when you have "Print" chose, you can pick "Shading" or "Example," and you'll have the option to alter more.

*Select All - A standard altering device to choose every one of the components/layers without a moment's delay in the material area.*

*Edit - A method for cutting stuff from the material, duplicate a component, or glue components.* It's basically equivalent to in a Word archive or photograph altering software.

*Align - Align stuff to some side in the material region.* It helps keep everything decent and organized.

*Arrange -* Move stuff behind or in front of other elements, i.e. you want a piece of text on top of a shape, and not halfway hidden behind it.

*Flip - Quickly flip components evenly or vertically.*

*Size - All components have size, and with this symbol, you can change the width and tallness.* Aspects will forever be a similar when the little lock is on.

*Rotate - Move a component around to various points as you like.*

*Position - This lets you know where your components are on the material's x-y grid.*

*Font - Choose your textual style.* Except if you purposefully need to purchase a Cricut font,
ensure you're utilizing ones that are free.

*Style - a similar symbol in Word, style simply allows you to pick assuming you need your text style bolded, emphasized, etc.*

*Font size, letter space, line space - These three capacities let you pick the size of your textual style, how much space is in the middle of each letter, and how much space is in the middle of section lines.*

*Alignment - This symbol applies to the arrangement of paragraphs.*

*Curve - Curve your text around up or down, or even into a circle.*

*Advance - This one is somewhat peculiar.* At the point when you click on it, you'll see three choices: ungroup to letters, ungroup to lines, and ungroup to layers. Ungroup to letters implies each letter turns into its own layers. You would tap on this to change each single letter. You type your passage, click ungroup to lines, and presently your section is isolated into individual lines you can alter. The ungroup to layers just applies to multi-facet text styles, which you need to purchase. For instance, a few extravagant textual styles will have a shadow or additional layer, yet assuming you would rather not the shadow or additional part, you can click ungroup to layers to isolate them, and afterward erase the shadow.

<u>Left</u>

Time to move to the left board. Here you can add plans like shapes and pictures. How about we go through the seven symbols quickly:

*New - Create a new project.*

*Templates - See a layout on sorts of stuff you can cut (like a format for a sack bag).*

*Projects - See extends all set and cut on Cricut Access (which you really want a membership for), however some are accessible free of charge, to spend more cash than what you're paying for your subscription.*
*Images - See pictures (some of which are free) accessible on Cricut Access or cartridges.*

*Text - Add text to the material area.*

*Shapes - Add shapes to the material area.*
*Upload - Upload your own pictures for nothing, no membership*

*required.* <u>Right</u>

The right board is about layers. The most straightforward undertakings can have as not many as one layer, while complex ones will have various layers. For instance, assuming you're planning a sticker that is looking like a star, since you'll utilize yellow-shaded sticker paper, that is only one layer. Notwithstanding, with different tasks, there will be different components, and every one of those is a different layer.
Let's investigate the board's icons:

*Group - Click this to bunch various components/layers together so they're more straightforward to work with.*

*Ungroup - Ungroup components you've assembled to alter every component individually*

*Duplicate - Duplicate a chose component, so there's presently two of them.*

*Delete - Remove any chose elements.*

*Linetype/fill - When a layer is chosen, look to this symbol to see what you're utilizing (cut, compose, score, etc).*

*Layer perceivability - This symbol allows you to turn components imperceptible rather than erasing them, so you can choose if you need to keep it or not.*

*Blank material - This allows you to change the shade of your canvas.*

*Slice - Cut out components (shapes, message, and so forth) you like from various designs.*

*Weld - Combine layers (there is no "unweld" function).*

*Attach - Keeps layers together on the material and when you send it to cut.*

*Flatten - Used with the Print then, at that point, Cut capacity, Flatten will mush numerous layers into one to be printed and afterward cut.* This can't be undone.

*Contour - Hide specific pieces of your design.*

*Color sync - All tones on the material address an alternate material,* so assuming that you needn't bother with numerous shades of, say, red, you can snap and drag the shade you don't need, and afterward drop it on the one you would like to utilize, so you just have

one red. This implies you'll utilize less material when cutting time comes.

And that is essentially all that you want to be familiar with Design Space's icons!

**Design Space app**

What assuming you're utilizing Cricut's Design Space application, which is accessible for the two iOs and Android? How could it be unique? Reply: It isn't actually unique. It's simply organized a piece distinctively to fit more modest screens. The symbols generally mean exactly the same things. Exploring will be somewhat unique, since you're utilizing your fingertips. Here are the controls:

To choose a picture, tap once with your

finger. To choose more than one picture,
swipe.
To move around the material, utilize two fingers.
To zoom out and see everything on the material, twofold tap.
To zoom in and out, squeeze with your thumb and record
finger.

There are sure highlights just accessible on the full work area adaptation, similar to bend text; ungrouping textual styles to lines when there's a section; formats; and examples. In any case, you can utilize the application disconnected, and there's an element called SnapMat. Utilizing your camera, you can snap a photo of the material you're utilizing on your mat, and afterward orchestrate your plan over it so you can perceive how it will examine genuine life.

**Uploading your first images**

If you're feeling overpowered by every one of the symbols and what they mean, that is OK! Careful discipline brings about promising results with Design Space, and until you get a couple of ventures added to your repertoire, it's typical for everything to feel pretty befuddling. Before we get into the instructional exercises for explicit undertakings, how about we really accomplish something with it. How about we transfer an image.

First, download a picture you need to use to your PC, regardless of whether it's a free drawing from a blog, a unique outline, or whatever.

<u>Image types</u>

Images are generally in JPG, PNG, or SVG record designs. JPG isn't the most ideal decision for Design Space, since that sort isn't truly adaptable. Configuration Space upholds them, yet for the time being, it's ideal to keep away from them. A PNG with a straightforward foundation is great, and assuming you get your picture from a blog, they will undoubtedly have saved it in PNG or SVG. What's a SVG? It's a vector picture, and it's the best kind for Design Space. These are extremely straightforward and simple to alter. They can likewise be resized without losing quality. If conceivable, consistently attempt to utilize SVG images.

When you transfer your picture, you'll be approached to choose in the event that the picture is "Straightforward," "Decently Complex," or "Complex." Cricut shows an illustration of what they mean for each sort. Assuming your picture is mind boggling, similar to a photograph, hitting "Straightforward" really adjusts what it resembles. You might need this, so click on the three to see what it does to picture, and make your choice.

<u>Removing elements</u>

Make your selection, then hit continue. On the upper left of the screen, you'll see three symbols: an enchanted wand, an eraser, and the harvest box. Assuming your picture has a foundation and you don't need that remembered for your finished product, you can dispose of it with the enchanted wand. Click the foundation. Assuming you see a checkerboard instead of the first foundation, you've effectively taken out the background.

The thing with the enchanted wand is that it eliminates everything like what you select; for more explicit expulsions, you would utilize the eraser. To perceive how Cricut will cut the plan in its present status, hit "Review" on the lower part of the

screen. <u>Saving the</u>

<u>image</u>

To save the image, you'll be given the option of saving as a "Print then Cut" or a regular "Cut." If your picture needn't bother with shading and you're not anticipating printing it first, save as "Cut." Add labels (this is the main time you can do this), so you can without much of a stretch observe the picture when you want it for a task. In the following section, we're going to walkthrough what to do to Print then Cut.

## Chapter 4: Making Stickers and Decals

Making your own stickers is one of the best time projects with Cricut. Regardless of whether you're an instructor who needs a cool method for denoting understudies' work; a functioning journaler who needs a vivid method for remaining coordinated; or an expert craftsman sharing their work in a reasonable structure, stickers are incredible. In this chapter, we're going over Print then Cut stickers; vinyl window decals; and wall decals.

### Stickers

Making stickers is the ideal method for getting to realize the Print Then Cut capacity, which is perhaps the coolest thing about Cricut. You can make a colorful, patterned design in Design Space, then send it your home printer for printing. Everything is now set up and Cricut perceives the plan precisely as it shows up on the page, so it's ready to cut it precisely. We should stroll through the process.

<u>Get the right materials</u>

For Print then Cut stickers, you need the right paper and printer. Cricut suggests 8.5 x 11-inch white materials. The maximum image size for Print then Cut, however, will be 9.25 x 6.75-inches, so remember that when planning. White printable sticker paper is the best approach, which you can find in make stores and on the Cricut website.

As for the printer, it truly matters. There are inkjet printers and laser printers. Which one you need relies upon your inclination and financial plan; simply ensure you're utilizing the right kind of sticker paper for your particular printer type. On their site, Cricut does recommend an inkjet printer for all Print then Cut projects (not just stickers) with the Explore series.

<u>Sticker with no additional elements</u>

Upload the image you want as your sticker and save it as a Print then Cut. On the off chance that you have Cricut access, there are a great many choices, a significant number of which are free. Assuming the picture you pick is the main thing you need on your sticker (no additional components like words), the interaction is straightforward. Once you've selected the save as Print then Cut, name the image and add tags. Start another venture and add the image.

Now, you're in the Design Space material region. Since this is all you need to Print then, at that point, Cut, you can feel free to click "Make It."

A review will spring up. On the following screen, you'll be incited to choose your Printer. You need picture drain ON. This guarantees that you don't wind up with small amounts of white edging on your end result. Print, and afterward place the paper on the Cricut cutting mat and feed into the machine. "Printable Sticker Paper" is a custom setting, so assuming you're utilizing a Cricut investigate, turn the smart

dial to "Custom." Select "Peruse All Materials," and observe the sticker paper setting. For Makers, there's no dial; you simply pick the material in Design Space.

Make sure the sticker paper is straight, and that the edge is adjusted in the upper left corner straightforwardly along the upper left edge of the mat. Cricut needs the paper straight and perfectly located to output and afterward cut the imprints accurately. For the best outcomes, you ought to consistently attempt to cut just after you print.

<u>Sticker with added elements</u>

If you need to add more components to your sticker, the cycle makes a couple of more strides. What different components may you add? Anything you need, similar to shapes or text. Suppose you need text imprinted on the picture, yet at the same not cut out. You can utilize the add text symbol, compose what you need, and orchestrate it inside the picture's limits. Select All and afterward Flatten, so the sticker is every one of the one layer.

If you need your picture on top of another shape (you may need this assuming your picture is really a word or series of words), you click on the Shapes symbol and pick which one you need. It will be dark, since Design Space thinks you simply need to cut it at the present time, not print. To fill it with a shading or example, select it and hit "fill for print," and afterward the shading or print type. Make your determination, and afterward move your text picture on top, so it's the place where you need it to be. Assuming that the circle is in front, right snap and hit "move forward."

If you're content with your sticker configuration, straighten the entire thing to one layer, so Cricut realizes you will send it to print first. Ensure the absolute size is no greater than 9.25 x 6.75 inches. Inside that size, you can copy your sticker assuming you need. Now, click "Make It" and finish printing, then put into your Cricut for cutting.

<u>Stickers without Print then Cut</u>

If your sticker doesn't need to be printed first (i.e. you have a patterned or solid-colored sticker paper you want to use), you won't be going through the whole Print then Cut process. You save the image you want as a "Cut," design as you like, and hit "Make It." Be sure you have the material you want in your Cricut machine, and you've selected it at the "Make It" stage. If you're utilizing your sticker on a surface other than paper, similar to tempered steel or glass containers, removable vinyl is way better compared to sticker paper. You'll have the option to eliminate the vinyl on the off chance that you really want to.

**Blade settings**

Something last: edge settings. You get to these in the "Make It" stage, when you're concluding subtleties just prior to cutting. Cricut has a page ("Which materials would I be able to cut with my Cricut Explore and Maker machine?) on suggested cutting edge cut strain for materials. At the point when you're choosing a custom material, you'll see a dropdown menu for tension with choices for not so much, default, but rather more. Assuming your blade is somewhat dull, more tension is really smart. For more itemized settings, nonetheless, you can tap on the "material settings" on the base left of the screen. There are three settings there: cut strain, multi-cut, and cutting edge type. At the point when you have the settings you need for your material, make certain to save them.

**Vinyl window decals**

Making a vinyl window decal isn't vastly different than a customary sticker with regards to planning it in Design Space. The material is simply unique. A long-lasting outside vinyl is a decent decision in the event that you anticipate putting it on your vehicle, while removable vinyl is really great for indoor applications. Vector pictures are ideal for vinyl stickers, since they are simple.

Designing your window decal

Upload or pick your picture in Cricut Design. Assuming your picture has a foundation, eliminate it with the enchanted wand apparatus, ensuring you have that checkerboard design wherever you need it. Hit "Review" sometimes to perceive how your sticker is meeting up. You will be saving the picture you need as a "Cut" picture, since you're not printing anything first.

Now, go into another venture and add the picture you recently saved. Make any changes you need and afterward hit "Make It." Be certain to choose the right material and a kiss cut setting. Kiss slice will get the blade through the plan, yet it leaves the sponsorship material flawless. Any time you have a sponsorship material on your material, a kiss cut is a decent wagered. When the sticker is cut, it's an ideal opportunity to weed. Weeding is the most common way of eliminating vinyl pieces not piece of the plan. Cricut has an exceptional apparatus for this, and assuming that you anticipate making stuff like stickers and stencils, it's very useful.

Applying the decal

To apply the decal, you need to ensure the window you're applying on is perfect. Clean with scouring liquor, since a window cleaning item can leave behind buildup that makes it harder for the decal to stick. Air dry the glass. Now, with something like a scrubber or a Visa, rub it at the edge of the decal with the reasonable tape to eliminate any air bubbles. Start from one edge and go to the other.

Put a layer of Transfer Tape, which you can get from Circuit, on top of your decal. This tape is truly useful while putting your vinyl. Then, strip back the paper sponsorship, and start applying the decal where you need it. Start with

one corner and move cautiously, so it doesn't move. With your charge card or scrubber, smooth over the decal again to eliminate any wanderer bubbles. To finish the interaction, strip back your exchange tape, however some people
suggest keeping it on for 24 hours, so the vinyl part truly sets and sticks. When stripping the exchange tape, be exceptionally delicate, or you may pull the entire decal off.

**Wall decals**

Making a divider decal is the same than a window decal - you simply stick it on your divider rather than your window or vehicle. Nonetheless, you need to make certain to utilize removable vinyl, since sooner or later, you will most likely need to eliminate the decal assuming you move or need to paint that wall.

Designing, cutting, and applying a divider decal is basically the same as a window decal. Periodically, however, a divider decal is a lot greater. Now, you have a bit more space than with your Print then Cut stickers (you will have 12 x 24- inches to work with), but if your wall decal is big, you're going to get an error message. The undertaking won't cut. You simply need to advise the Cricut to cut specific parts on isolated mats, and afterward you gather everything into one place yourself on the wall.

Selecting portions of the enormous image

Click on Shapes and make a square shape that is inside the size of the mat, so 11-inches wide and 22-inches high. Contingent upon the shape and accurate size of your too-enormous layer, your square shapes could be more modest, and they might be squares. However long they are each inside the mat size, it's fine.

Duplicate that square shape however many occasions depending on the situation until they cover your large picture, with no cross-over. Outwardly, this is the way the layer will be cut into mat-sized pieces, however Cricut doesn't realize that is the thing that you need to do. Select every one of the square shapes and send them in reverse, so you can see your huge layer on top.

Isolating the ideal layer

Select one of the square shapes and your huge layer, and snap "Cut." Every time you cut, the new layers shoot up to the highest point of your layer board for simple altering. There will be layers that are something similar, and you simply need one of these. You can likewise erase the square shape, since it has filled its need. When you've cut your new layer that you need Cricut to cut, it's really smart to change its tone, to make sure you can remain coordinated and see what you've as of now cut. Rehash this cycle with every one of the square shapes until the whole of your enormous layer is split into mat-sized pieces. You are presently ready to cut your plan without a mistake message.

## Chapter 5: Making Cards

You can undoubtedly make cards utilizing a couple of capacities on the Cricut. In principle, all you really want to do it have the machine cut a card-molded piece of paper for you. For greater frivolity, you can utilize the Cricut to remove various shapes, and afterward you orchestrate them as you like on your cut card as it was done in the good 'ol days. In this part, we will stroll through some further developed card-production strategies, such as making a scored card, a molded card, and card with text and example utilizing the Print Then Cut function.

**Scoring tools**

When Cricut scores a card, it's fundamentally adding twist lines, so it's not difficult to overlay the card in an orderly fashion in a particular spot. To score, Cricut utilizes a unique apparatus: the Scoring Stylus. Assuming you have a Cricut Explore One, you additionally need the Accessory Adapter, which is intended for adding pens, as well. To involve the pointer in Explore One, you really want to open the clasp and eliminate the cutting edge and lodging. Put the pointer in the connector and hold the brace up, pushing it down into the holder. It will click. Close the clip. The connector is just for the Explore One.

The Explore Air and Air 2 have their own clips separate from the sharp edge. You simply open up the frill cinch and hold it up while driving the pointer into the holder. It will click and be secure. The most up to date Cricut, the Maker, likewise utilizes the pointer, however there's one more instrument for scoring: the scoring wheel.
Bought independently, the wheel has multiple times the tension of the pointer, so it very well may be utilized on a lot more materials. There's one lodging for the wheel, and two wheels, one which has a solitary roller, the other which has two. Contingent upon the material, you'll be asked by Design Space to trade out roller 01 or 02. On the off chance that you're utilizing the Maker and don't have a wheel, click "Alter Tools" to choose the stylus.

**Basic plain card with score**

Let's get into the card plan. On the off chance that you need simply a plain, clear card with a score line, the interaction is really simple. You'll be advising the Cricut to remove a piece of paper in the size you need for your card, and afterward adding a score line.

First, open up Design Space and start another task. Then, click on "Shapes" and select the square. To open the extents, click on the little lock in the Size board (where the width and stature are estimated), so you can meddle with the extents as you like.

When making your card shape, recall that you'll be collapsing it down the middle, so a 10 x 7-inch square shape is in all actuality a 5 x 3.5-inch card. When you have your card shape, it's an ideal opportunity to add your score line. Click on "Shapes" and select Option Score line. At the point when this is chosen and you click in your material region, an upward (it's vertical as a matter of course) ran line shows up. This ran line is advising your Cricut to score, and not cut. Size the line so it squeezes into your square shape. Then, select both and adjust them from the top board. Presently, you really want to append the square shape and score line together. Select both on your material region and snap "Connect," which you can find on the right board, which is the Layers board. Click "Make It," select the right material, and you're great to go!

**Shaped cards with score**

What in the event that you need your card in a particular shape, and in addition to a square shape or square? Cricut can more than handle that. Suppose you need to make a heart-molded Valentine for someone. There's a heart shape accessible in the "Shapes." Remember, you really need two hearts, since it will be collapsed. To get them adjusted accurately, select one of the hearts and snap "Flip" and afterward "Flip Vertical."

Next, move the hearts so they're covered a little on their awe-inspiring finishes (not the sharp end), and afterward adjust to focus flat. You ought to have a typical heart sitting on your material, and afterward above it, scarcely contacting, a topsy turvy heart.

Right now, Cricut considers these two hearts to be two separate shapes. You need the machine to consider them to be one shape, or they will be cut separated. To do that, you will choose the two heart layers and utilize the Weld symbol on the lower part of the layers board. When welded, the two hearts are currently really one shape. The advantage of this welding is that regardless of whether you have a scoring apparatus, Cricut can cut the card for you as one shape, and you can overlap it yourself. Assuming you in all actuality do have a scoring device, however, add the line by tapping on Shapes and afterward the Score line. Like previously, it's vertical of course, so you need to choose the score line and pivot it 90-degrees.

To unite everything, select your welded heart and the score line, then, at that point, focus adjust them, and append. Click "Make It," select the material you're utilizing, and Cricut will get to work.

**Making a card with Print then Cut**

Let's say you needed to print a designed card, and afterward have the Cricut cut and compose on it for you. You can do this with any card with an essential rectangular/square shape or a more exceptional shape, similar to our heart card from a higher place. Since we just found out with regards to the heart card, how about we utilize that as our springboard. Presently, how the heart looks like relies upon the paper you use. We can change that assuming we print it out first with an example or picture. Then, Cricut can score, cut, and write on the card for you, assuming you have the necessary tools.

Designing the card

For this card, it's ideal to begin without any preparation, so start with another undertaking. Add the shape you need, similar to the heart, and afterward add another. Flip, adjust, and weld like previously, so you have one shape. Presently, fill the shape with a shading or example you like utilizing the Fill instrument. To add, similar to more shapes or pictures, feel free to add them now. When your visual components are great, add a score line and adjust appropriately, yet don't really join it yet. We will add text first.

Click the text symbol in the left board. It makes a difference what textual style you use, on the grounds that main Cricut text styles can get you that composing impact, your System text styles will not. With System text styles, Cricut does this thing where the composing seems illustrated, and not transcribed. Assuming that is the thing that you need, that is fine, yet for a transcribed look, you need to utilize Cricut textual styles. These require a Cricut Access membership and they cost cash, however you presumably have a few example text styles you could utilize. Under the textual style menu, ensure the text has a "expressing" choice, and select it. Play with the textual style utilizing instruments like letter separating, bend, and more to get the style you want.

Printing, scoring, drawing, and cutting

Once you're content with your text, you can choose every one of the components and snap Attach. This is a vital stage, so remember it. *Presently,* you can proceed to click "Make It." This card has four stages: printing, scoring, drawing, and cutting. Check out the see cautiously so you know what the means are and assuming you really want to make any changes, similar to where the plan is on the canvas.

Click "Proceed" and follow the instructions.

Printing starts things out, so your printer ought to be on, associated with your PC, and stacked with the right material. Once printed, you'll be approached to choose your material. Assuming that you have an Explore, you'll have to move the savvy dial to the right material, however with a Maker, you simply select the right one on the PC. Then, load the mats and apparatuses. Stay close by, in light of the fact that eventually, Cricut will request that you trade an apparatus out for one more one.

**Making envelopes**

Need a custom envelope for your custom card? The Cricut can make those, as well. It's least demanding on the off chance that you have Cricut Access. In the first place, open another undertaking. Then, click on Images, and in the search bar, search for "envelope." There will be heaps of choices, including something like one free one, so pick the plan you like. Ponder the state of your card (square shape, square, or more remarkable shape) and which style of envelope would work best. At the point when the envelope configuration is embedded into your plan region, you'll see score lines. Once printed, you'll have the option to overlap your envelope.

To ensure your envelope fits the card you have as a top priority, you're really going to embed only the state of your card into the material region for reference; you don't need to plan the entire thing again or anything. Keep in mind, to make the specific size and shape you need, open the extents. At this moment, the envelope will presumably be excessively little for the card, so presently it's an ideal opportunity to measure the envelope. Put the card shape over the envelope for reference, so you realize you'll get an ideal fit. You can open the extents of the envelope if necessary.

What sort of paper material would it be advisable for you to use for an envelope? An option that could be more slender than cardstock is appropriately best, similar to a normal piece of printer paper or shaded development paper. At the point when you click "Make It" on your envelope, focus on how huge it is and assuming it fits on the 12 x 12 mat, or then again on the off chance that you will require the greater 12 x 24. Load your mat and material, and feel free to cut your envelope!

## Chapter 6: Vinyl Stencils and Iron-On Vinyl

Vinyl materials aren't restricted to window and decals. You can utilize them to make stencils for an assortment of ventures (signs, banners, painted pad cases, and so on) and iron-on plans for a wide range of apparel and even wood. In this part, we'll stroll through how to make a vinyl stencil and iron-on.

### Stencils

Making a stencil is actually somewhat easy or not the same as different kinds of vinyl decals. Be that as it may, rather than cutting around your plan or letters, a stencil should be planned so Cricut removes within part, and not the layout. Suppose you need to paint a statement on something, similar to a wooden sign or cushion. Open another task and pick your textual style. Compose your statement, utilizing another text block for each new line of text.

<u>Designing</u>

If you're utilizing a Script textual style, you will most likely need to draw the letters nearer together, so select the text, ungroup, and afterward move the letters around however you would prefer. Presently, you need to weld them, so select the message and hit the weld icon.

When you like how your message looks, connect the entirety of the message. Assuming you were utilizing a picture, similar to a SVG, simply embed it into your undertaking as opposed to composing your text. Size (either the text or the picture) to your liking.

Now, it's time to create the stencil part of the design. Click Shapes and select the square. You will probably need to make a rectangle, so click the lock to unlock the proportions. Now is a good time to do so more sizing - stretch the rectangle to those dimensions, whether it's a pillowcase, wooden sign, bag front, T-shirt front, etc. Click "Move to Back" on the shape, so you can actually see the text or image over it. To make things easier, you can change the text or image color, so it's easier to see. Size the text or image, making sure it stays within the shape. Now, Cricut knows to cut out the letters.

<u>Loading the materials</u>

Cricut stencil vinyl is a great material to use for stencils. It has framework lines and clings well to an assortment of base materials, so you don't need to stress over your stencil slipping around while you're attempting to paint. The cement likewise forestalls paint dying. The one disadvantage is that stencil vinyl is expected for a one-time frame use. At the point when your configuration is all set, hit "Make It" and afterward pick the stencil vinyl material. Assuming that you have an Explore, you'll have to move the shrewd dial to "custom."

Painting

Once your stencil is cut, it's an ideal opportunity to weed. You'll eliminate the letters or within the actual picture. Apply Cricut's exchange tape over the stencil, utilizing the matrix lines as direction. Get the base material out (pillowcase, sign, and so on) and apply the stencil on like you would an ordinary vinyl on a window or divider. Then, cautiously eliminate the exchange paper. It isn't as large of an arrangement assuming the edges fire coming up in places, on the grounds that the stencil won't be for all time on your task, however you actually need it stuck safely, so it remains straight while you paint.

Once the exchange paper is off, it's an ideal opportunity to paint. Touch the paint cautiously, instead of brushing. Ensure you're utilizing a paint that was intended for the base material. Strip the stencil off while the paint is as yet wet. Dry completely. In the event that you were painting on a pillowcase or other texture, it's additionally really smart to go over the paint with an iron utilizing light pressure.

**Iron-on vinyl**

Creating plans for iron-on vinyl is basically the same as planning a window or divider decal. Gather the pictures you need to use for your iron-on vinyl fixes or fixes. Like with decals, straightforward vector (SVG) pictures are ideal, regardless of whether it's text style or portrayal of something, similar to a creature, tree, unique plan, what have you. Put the pictures on your material and resize fittingly dependent on what you anticipate pressing them on to. On the off chance that you don't know, feel free to quantify the thing (a T-shirt, pack front, and so forth) and afterward size your plan in Design Space.

If you are printing various plans on the double, ensure they're a similar shading. Despite the fact that these plans will not really be in shading since you're not printing them first, having them be generally similar advises Cricut to remove them on a similar mat, so you utilize less material. Assuming every one of your plans together are too huge for the mat, nonetheless, Cricut will likewise tell you, and you can simply anticipate removing them on isolated mats to keep them that big.

Once you're content with the plan and its size, click "Make It." This part is significant: you need to click "Mirror" on the see screen's sidebar. Otherwise, your picture will wind up in reverse when you're attempting to press it on. For ordinary iron-on material, Cricut will likewise advise you to stack it sparkling side down on the mat. Select the material you're utilizing and, assuming you have an Explore, turn the shrewd dial to the right setting, also. For regular iron-on, a fine-point sharp edge is recommended.

**Application**

Once the plan is cut, you'll have to weed. Cricut makes an exceptional apparatus for weeding, and assuming you've made window or divider decals, you are most likely intimately acquainted with it. All iron-on materials use heat, however the specific guidelines can fluctuate contingent upon the material you're utilizing. How about we stroll through a portion of the well known sorts: regular iron on, sparkle iron-on, holographic, and designed iron-on.

Everyday iron-on (it used to be called iron-on light, however Cricut supplanted it with the ordinary iron-on material) is an adaptable material that chips away at most base materials, including most textures and even wood. Before you even start the interaction, you need to pre-wash whatever you're applying your vinyl to.
Companies normally treat their garments with different synthetic compounds to make the shadings pop, and they should be eliminated. Regardless of whether the thing you're applying to has been washed previously, simply feel free to give it a wash and dry anyway.
You would rather not make a difference your fix to messy fabric.

If you're involving a normal iron for your application, you need it on high hotness, however no steam, so ensure the iron is totally dry. Assuming that you're utilizing the Cricut EasyPress machine, set it to 315-degrees for regular iron on. For your squeezing surface, it ought to be level, firm, and around midsection tallness. Assuming you're worried that applying a lot of tension will make the surface breakdown, don't utilize it.

Press around the base material with the iron or EasyPress for a couple of moments to smooth it out. Then, you will put a slender piece of cotton material between the vinyl and iron. This guarantees no coincidental softening happens. Press the fix against your base material, holding down with firm tension for 15-30 seconds. Assuming the fix is bigger than your iron, you will push down in stages; don't slide the iron around, in light of the fact that this doesn't allow the vinyl really to follow, you're simply warming it up.

Once you're squeezed all over, pause. The lingering heat allows the vinyl the best opportunity of truly staying. When the vinyl is cool, go on and cautiously strip back the exchange sheet. Assuming the entire fix begins accompanying it, lay it back down and rehash it with the hot iron. Stand by 24 hours prior to washing the thing once more, and from now on, consistently wash it back to front on a delicate setting.

*One more tip on ordinary iron: don't layer it over sparkle iron-on.* Notwithstanding, holographic, sparkle, foil, holographic shimmer, and sparkle network materials might be layered over regular iron on.

<u>Glitter iron-on</u>

Glitter iron-on gives your undertaking a particular glittery, glossy look. Assuming you're putting it on texture, wash it as you would with regular iron. Assuming that you're utilizing a normal iron, set it to the most noteworthy temperature setting, with no steam. For the EasyPress, it relies upon what your base material is. Cricut has a hotness guide where you select what the base is, and it gives you guidelines. For instance, on the off chance that you're applying sparkle iron-on to 100 percent cotton (and you're utilizing the EasyPress mat also), set the EasyPress to 330-degrees and apply light tension for 30 seconds. Once applied, stand by 24 hours prior to washing the item.

Glitter network is viewed as an alternate sort of material and has a more lattice like appearance. The hotness suggestions are something similar, however.

<u>Holographic</u>

Cricut suggests utilizing holographic iron-on for white materials for the best outcome. In the event that there's one more tone behind it, the holographic may not appear as though what you needed. While applying this sort of iron on, keep similar guidelines as usual: wash the thing, pick a level, firm surface, and preheat the base material with your iron or EasyPress. This time, in any case, you will set the iron to the "Fleece" setting, or around 330-degrees on the EasyPress with the mat. No steam, as usual.

<u>Patterned iron-on</u>

For more tone, designed iron-on vinyl is an incredible decision. It feels somewhat not quite the same as different sorts of vinyl, yet applies essentially the same way. In the event that you're utilizing an ordinary iron, utilize the Cotton setting with the steam off. In the event that you're utilizing your EasyPress, go to the Interactive Heat Guide to track down the right setting for the base material. For cotton, it's 340-degrees. You need to make certain to allow the vinyl to cool totally prior to stripping back the exchange sheet.

## Chapter 7: Drawing Coloring Books And Illustration  Cards

Creating your own shading book pages and cards is easy with a Cricut. Hand crafted, tweaked shading books are an incredible gift thought for the youngsters in your day to day existence, or the grown-ups. Shading books aren't age-confined. Assuming you add text for Cricut to draw, too, you get a shading book that is additionally a story book. To shading in a card or simply get a cool representation look, the interaction is fundamentally equivalent to a shading book page. There's a ton you can do with the Cricut's capacity to draw, yet making shading books and outlined cards is a truly genuine illustration of that capacity in action.

### Choosing pens and paper

Pens matter with regards to drawing. For a standard shading page, you will likely need to go with dark, yet how thick do you need the lines to be? Cricut sells an assortment, so ponder the look you need. For a more adult shading book or a pleasant card, little tipped pen widths look great. Cricut even sells a calligraphy style pen, which is incredible for composing script texts. *Similarly as a FYI, it should be introduced at a 45-degree point. There's a triangle on the pen's body that demonstrates the establishment heading.* Cricut doesn't provide you with a see of what the tips resemble, so you'll need to do some experimenting.

Coloring books or cards don't need to be just in dark, so think about utilizing colors, particularly for cards. There are additionally metallic and sparkle pens, which can be utilized with strong shadings for a truly cool look.

As for paper, smooth watercolor paper is an extraordinary decision for shading books. For cards, whatever you for the most part use for standard cards is fine, however sparkle and metallic pens look great on shinier paper since they don't seep through. Metallic pens in splendid tones ought to be utilized on dim cardstock.

### Designing

First, it's an ideal opportunity to get the picture you need to draw.

You preferably need a solitary layer, yet assuming the picture you pick has different layers, you can choose the picture and over on Layers, change every one to the composing capacity. This is likewise an opportunity to pick your pen type (fine point, gel, and so forth) and shading. You ought to clearly just pick the shades of pens that you really have. It doesn't really make any difference what type and shading you pick inside Design Space, the Cricut won't realize what you're really utilizing, however it's exceptionally helpful to remain coordinated. As a FYI, your lines won't appear to be unique in Design Space dependent on the pen type you pick.

If you see lines crossing one another and you don't need that look, you can go in, ungroup the picture, and eliminate any layers you don't need. To pull together the picture layers, just "draw" a container around everything (snap and drag, the case is in reality a feature, not a genuine shape), and hit "Gathering." Then, feature everything once more, and hit "Attach."

If you need to keep things truly straightforward, you can really observe bunches of pictures on Cricut Access that will naturally be put on your material region prepared for drawing. You won't have to do a ton of altering or tidying up. Look into the expression "draw" in the Image search bar.

**Sizing your coloring book/card**

The subsequent stage is to conclude how large you need the shading book pages or card to be. Pick a shape from the Shapes symbol - you'll likely need a square - and afterward open the extents. Contingent upon your undertaking, you might need another shape, so pick the one you need. Every one of the accompanying guidelines actually apply. Stretch it to the size and shape you need. The shade of the shape doesn't make any difference, however a many individuals like to make it the shading the material they're utilizing, to make sure they get a more precise look. Ensure the linetype is set to "Cut" and "No Fill."

For shading books, on the off chance that your shape is on the little side, you could possibly get one more page cut out from a similar mat of material. Copy the shape and make it a similar shading, so Cricut kPresentlys to remove it on a similar piece of material. You can copy the shape for however many pages as you need; simply change the shading when you run out of mat space, so Cricut realizes you need to remove it on an alternate mat. Now, move the drawing pictures you planned onto your shape(s). Twofold check and ensure the line type says "draw" for each picture.

Add text now, assuming that is important for your ideal plan. In the event that you need the textual style to be composed and not illustrated, ensure the text is set to "Stating" in the textual style menu. Just certain textual styles have this choice. Assuming you need the text illustrated, so it tends to be shaded in also, you're really going to return up to Linetype and pick "draw," instead of "cut."

Next, you will rehash that featuring thing and feature a crate around the shading book page, picture, and text, in the event that you have any. Connect everything. This is significant; it tells Cricut you need it to remove a shape, and draw on that equivalent shape. Rehash for each page and its image.

**Cutting and drawing**

Once your configuration is all set, it's an ideal opportunity to "Make It." Set your material to the right paper and ensure your cutting blade and the right pen (Cricut will let you know which one to do first, on the off chance that you're utilizing products) are both stacked into the machine. Cricut will likewise let you know when to switch pens, assuming that you're utilizing various shadings and types. To this end it's so helpful to pick the right pen type and shading for all your drawing/composing lines back in the planning stage. Load your paper and watch the cycle. Once everything is drawn and cut, let the ink dry. That is it!

## Chapter 8: Tips, Tricks, and Hacks

When it comes to Cricut machines, careful discipline brings about promising results. Notwithstanding, as you go through different ventures, there are tips, deceives, and hacks that can assist with making the interaction more straightforward. In this section, we'll go through probably the best ones we found on different web journals, similar to "The Homes I Have Made," "Sweet Red Poppy," "The Crafted Sparrow," and "Jennifer Maker." Here's what to be familiar with instruments, mats, Design Space, and the interaction after cutting.

**Tools**

Tools like the right edges and pens guarantee each venture turns out only the manner in which you need it. Here are a few hints on taking advantage of them:

<u>Keep separate cutting edges for your materials</u>

The standard Cricut sharp edges can cut an assortment of materials, yet to keep them in the most ideal shape, consider having committed edges for explicit materials. Which means, keep one sharp edge you utilize just for paper, one for vinyl, and one for texture. Along these lines, nobody edge will get abused and dull in a brief time of time.

<u>Get a cutting edge that slices thick materials</u>

Notwithstanding the standard sharp edge that accompanies your Cricut machine, having one explicitly intended to cut thicker material is a truly smart thought. Certain individuals observe that despite the fact that a standard edge ought to have the option to cut something, it gets found out or tears. Having a heavier-obligation cutting edge guarantees everything gets cut well. For the Explore series, get the profound cut cutting edge. With the Maker, the blade cutting edge is the one you'll want.

Sharpen dull blades

As your edges get more blunt, they won't cut too. Fortunately, you can hone them and expand their life expectancy a piece. You'll require uncompromising aluminum foil. Tear a sheet and burden it on a mat in your Cricut machine. In Design Space, set up a cut for certain circles, squares, and a few straight lines. Try to utilize the customary normal speed (not quick mode, assuming that is a choice), or the honing won't fill in as well.

Try out non-Cricut pens

Cricut pens can get costly, yet you can really utilize non-Cricut pens with progress. Bloggers have evaluated a pack and discovered some that work, for example, a
0.4 tip gelly roll metallic gel pen, Sharpie fine-point pens, Sharpie super fine point pens, Crayola super tip, Crayola almost negligible difference marker, and that's just the beginning. To embed a non-Cricut pen, hold a specialty stick (extravagant name for popsicle stick) under the cinch while you're placing in the pen. At the point when the tip of the pen scarcely contacts the specialty stick, close the cinch and attempt it out.

When finished with your venture, eliminate the pen

If your undertaking included pens, you need to make sure to eliminate the pen from the brace after you're finished. Set the cap back on. Assuming you fail to remember this progression, the pen will really dry out. At whatever point you complete a venture that pre-owned pens, make sure to take them out prior to proceeding with the remainder of your crafting.

**Mats**

Cutting mats are a fundamental piece of Cricut making. Without them, you can cut nothing. Assuming you use your machine a great deal, you'll go through mats before long, yet there are things you can do to make them last longer.

Get isolated mats for various materials

With specific materials, you truly do require various mats. Regardless of whether you use significantly unique material sorts, it's as yet really smart to get discrete mats for paper, vinyl, etc. Assuming you utilize glittery material, it's likewise really smart to utilize a mat only for those tasks, since the sparkle will probably adhere and be difficult to eliminate. Except if you need all that other material that goes on that mat to have a slender cleaning of sparkle, keep that one separate.

Keep the cover on the mats when you're not utilizing them

Cutting mats show up with a plastic cover for insurance. It's smart to hold tight to them, and when you're finished with your cutting, simply stick the cover back on. It shields the tacky surface from soil and debris.

Clean your mats

Your mats will get grimy, which makes them less tacky, so your materials won't remain secure when the Cricut cuts them. On the off chance that you utilize a mat a great deal for vinyl, felt, or texture, you likely can pull off utilizing tweezers to tidy up any small amounts and pieces. You can likewise move a build up roller on the mat. For a more profound clean, utilize a liquor free child wipe. For getting truly profound, you can really cover the mat in Goo Gone, let it sit for 15 minutes, and afterward scratch off all the messy glue with a scrubber instrument. On the off chance that you exceed all expectations, need to cover the mat with a splash glue, or it will not be tacky and can't be utilized once more. Dry completely before use.

Make sure you're involving the right mat for your material

The mat matters with regards to getting the right cuts. In the event that you utilize some unacceptable one, the material probably won't stick, stall excessively out, or get torn up by the sharp edge. The LightGrip mat is intended for scrapbook paper, crepe, tissue paper, and other slim materials. The StandardGrip is for cardstock, vinyl, and medium-weight. The StrongGrip is planned for thick cardstock, sparkle cardstock, calfskin, banner board, and other weighty materials. FOr FabricGrip
Mat is explicitly for textures like felt and cowhide on the Cricut Maker.

**Design Space**

The most significant and threatening piece of Cricut is presumably Design Space. Utilizing this product, you can make projects that are straightforward or exceptionally perplexing. Learning the in's and out's allows you to assemble your abilities. Here are some tips:

Start with the example project

To slip into utilizing Design Space and making, start with the example project the Cricut machine accompanies. Chances are, it will be a card. Before you attempt some other venture, attempt this one to plunge your toe into the water.

Use free pictures and text on Cricut Access

We truly suggest getting Cricut Access, which has a month to month (or yearly) expense. The advantage: to spend more cash, there are loads of free pictures and texts that Cricut offers Access endorsers. To set aside your cash for materials and instruments, utilize the free stuff however much as could be expected. Do some looking for bloggers offering free picture sets, as well.

Get the hang of search terms

When you're looking through the picture library, you utilize an inquiry bar and search terms. What words you use truly matters. Once in a while, even a truly conventional term will not create however many outcomes as you would might suspect, so analyze a little. Now and then it tends to be pretty much as basic as leaving an "s" off a term, such as looking into "envelope" rather than "envelopes." Search by equivalent word also, assuming you don't track down the thing you're searching for during your first search.

Look at pictures from a similar set/cartridge

When you're looking through pictures in Cricut Access, you may observe one to be that you truly like. To see more from a similar set or advanced cartridge, click on the little data circle (I) at the base right hand corner of the picture. The picture's subtleties will open up, with a green connection that takes you to the full picture set.

Upload free framework fonts

Design Space perceives your framework textual styles, and keeping in mind that they will not get that manually written look, they can be cut or illustrated. You can add to the variety of framework text styles through an assortment of sites like dafont.com,

1001freefonts.com, and that's only the tip of the iceberg. Note that the vast majority of these text styles are free for individual use. Assuming you anticipate selling any tasks with textual styles on them that are not public area, you'll need to pay for a business license.

Filter your picture searches

Looking for a particular kind of picture, similar to one with only one layer? There's a channel bar you can verify things in when you're placing in your hunt terms. Different channels are "type," like boundaries, outlines, foundations, and so on) and "proprietorship," as in Cricut Access, free, etc.

### Explore Ready-To-Make projects

If you don't know whether you have what it takes important to make a particular kind of venture or you need to investigate a comparative one first prior to making a plunge, look at Ready-To-Make projects on Design Space. These are accessible to Cricut Access individuals, and some of them are even free. Experts have planned these tasks, which shift from handbags to favor gift boxes, and that's only the tip of the iceberg. At the point when you select a Ready Make, you can see the guidelines and materials required, and you'll have the choice to go right to the "Make It" stage.

If you need to tweak, notwithstanding, hit the alter button. The design will then be sent to a new project and canvas, where you can edit any part of it. Be cautious about changing excessively, however, in the event that you're not exactly certain what it does. Altering a basic piece like aspects or ungrouping layers without refocusing them back may wreck things at the cutting stage, contingent upon the project.

### Use the Hide device to remain organized

When you're working with heaps of pictures, shapes, texts, and layers, the material region get jumbled before long. At the point when you're working one piece of your task, you can really conceal different layers by tapping on the little eye image close to those layers in the Layers Panel. They will vanish from the screen, however they're still there, so when you're prepared to see them once more, just hit the eye symbol again.

### When cutting complicated vinyl plans, make a weeding box

When your vinyl configuration is multifaceted, with bunches of little cuts, expect that
weeding can be interesting. Eliminating the pieces you don't need will require concentration, persistence, and a tweezer. To make things somewhat simpler for yourself, make a weeding box. This is only a square around your plan, and sent behind it. It makes the weeding system much easier.

**Cutting/Make It stage**

Once your configuration is done, you hit "Make It" and get taken to a mat review. There are still subtleties you can conclude here and settings to change. Here are a few hints on making your venture wonderful at this step:

<u>Do a test cut</u>

Technically, you do this prior to hitting "Make It" on your undertaking, yet this is a happy chance to do a test. A test cut will inform you as to whether you're involving the right blade and right cut tension for your material. Have your Cricut cut a little circle or another shape, so you know whether your blade is overcoming the material in the manner you want.

<u>Move pictures from mat to mat</u>

When no doubt about it "Make It" stage, you can really move pictures from one mat to another. For what reason would you need to do this? It can assist you with benefiting as much as possible from the space and save money on materials. To move an image, click on the 3 dots at its upper left-hand corner, then select "move to another mat."

<u>Favorite your most-utilized custom materials</u>

There are such countless materials in the Cricut, particularly the Maker, and looking through every one of them each an ideal opportunity to observe yours can get irritating. You would most loved the ones you be able to utilize the most, and under the Materials choice on the mat see, pick the "Top choices" envelope to rapidly get to the custom material you want.

<u>Use Fast Mode when you can</u>

The Cricut Explore Air 2 and Cricut Maker have a Fast Mode setting, what slices up to twice quicker than the normal setting. Remember, it's planned for Vinyl, Iron-On, and Cardstock materials. It works best with bigger plans, not more modest multifaceted ones, where tearing is possible with the higher cutting speed.

**After cutting**

Once you've cut your undertaking, there's regularly a ton of active work left to do, such as getting the material off the mat, weeding, and other gathering steps. Here are a few thoughts on making that interaction smoother:

<u>Use the right device to get the material off your mat</u>

When you've wrapped up cutting your task and are prepared to eliminate it, you may it truly adhered to the glue mat. Utilizing the freedoms devices forestalls tearing and tearing and disappointment. Cricut makes devices explicitly for this reason, similar to the scrubber and spatula. It's additionally really smart to make sure to strip the mat away from the venture, and not the reverse way around. Twist the mat away from your material. For little pieces, tweezers function admirably, too.

<u>Use a BrightPad for simple weeding</u>

Weeding vinyl and iron-ons can be interesting, particularly assuming your configuration is really nitty gritty. A BrightPad, which is essentially a level minimal light box, is an apparatus from Cricut that makes the cycle more straightforward. You lay your plan over it, and the light clarifies where you want to weed. To purchase an entire separate gadget, you can likewise set the plan against a window during the daytime for a comparable effect.

<u>Use a build up roller for cardstock weeding</u>

When you cut unpredictable plans on cardstock, weeding can be a genuine aggravation. Utilizing a couple of tweezers is the typical way, yet getting every single little piece can take forever.

For a lot quicker weeding meeting, utilize a build up roller. Prior to eliminating the plan from the mat, go over it with a build up roller to get the littlest pieces. You'll presumably still need to do somewhat seriously weeding, however you'll be beginning from a superior place.

<u>Get an EasyPress for iron-ons</u>

You in fact needn't bother with an EasyPress for applying iron-ons, you can pull off an iron, yet EasyPresses are planned explicitly for pressing on vinyl.

They are simpler to set and have a superior shape for pressing on. Since they are a

bit expensive, they will likely be generally valuable for individuals who do an adoration for iron-on vinyls. On the off chance that you just do a couple periodically, an EasyPress probably won't be an incredible investment.

<u>When collecting projects, organize everything simultaneously before gluing</u>

A ton of Cricut projects include removing a lot of plans and afterward gathering them in a scrapbook page, on a sack, or in cards.

Before you begin sticking or pressing on, consistently orchestrate everything on a superficial level region. Snap a photo so you remember where you put what, and afterward begin staying everything for real.

## Conclusion

Cricut machines can do three things: cut, draw, and when using the Print then Cut feature, basically print. With those three apparently straightforward assignments, you can open practically unlimited specialties and innovative undertakings. That is on account of the unbelievable force of Design Space, the cloud-based programming that Cricut employments. You can make cards, stickers, iron-on patches, shading books, thus substantially more. We scarcely contacted the surface on all that you can do.

So many individuals can profit from a Cricut machine, regardless of whether you anticipate making creates for gifts and your own home, or you need to sell what you make and need it to be up to proficient norms. There are so many ways you can utilize Design Space and with every one of the accessible materials and apparatuses like pens and sharp edges, unlimited ways of blending and-coordinate plans with various activities. You could involve a picture for a hello card, and afterward make it into a window decal. You could cut a plan on paper, and afterward, use it as an outline by changing the linetype from "cut" to "draw."

What's the key to capitalizing on your Cricut? Practice. All the task choices, materials, and apparatuses can get overpowering, and the best way to feel good is to rehearse. Start with basic ventures first, similar to the one that accompanies your recently bought Cricut machine. We've attempted to keep the vast majority of the walkthroughs in this book on the basic side, as well, so any of those is an incredible next specialty to try.

If you at any point wind up getting baffled or uncertain how to make what you need, do a little research on the web. There are such countless skilled makers out there who are sufficiently great to review itemized instructional exercises on pretty much every sort of undertaking, so assuming isn't in this book or you really want another point of view, find it. There are heaps of YouTube walkthroughs, also, to see and hear somebody disclosing what to do.

Even assuming you've never considered yourself "tricky," the Cricut can change that. In the event that removing things by hand is hard for you for wellbeing reasons, the Cricut is likewise a lifeline, and you can jump once more into creating without distress or agony. Cricut machines are tied in with changing a thought in your mind into something genuine and delightful. To release your inventiveness, think about Cricut.

www.ingramcontent.com/pod-product-compliance
Lightning Source LLC
Chambersburg PA
CBHW020520160726
47991CB00007B/3044